Permissions

Scripture quotations marked (NKJV) are taken from The New King James Version. ©1982 by Thomas Nelson, Nashville, TN, and are used by permission. Scripture quotations marked (NIV) are taken from the Holy Bible, New International Version®, NIV®. Copyright © 1973, 1978, 1984, 2011 by Biblica, Inc.™ Used by permission of Zondervan. All rights reserved worldwide. www. zondervan.com. The "NIV" and "New International Version" are trademarks registered in the United States Patent and Trademark Office by Biblica, Inc.™

The book title is a quotation by Rev. Dr. William Hiram Bentley, and is the motto of the National Black Evangelical Association (Chicago); see "Preface to the Second Edition," notes 3-4 in *The National Black Evangelical Association: Reflections on the Evolution of a Concept of Ministry* (Chicago: National Black Christian Students Conference, 1979, rev. ed.), 5-6, and is reprinted by permission of the National Black Evangelical Association and the author's estate via Ruth Lewis Bentley.

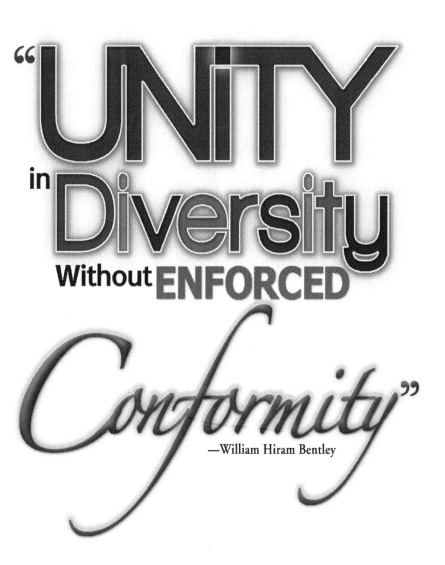

"UNITY in Diversity Without ENFORCED Conformity"

—William Hiram Bentley

REV. DR. WALTER ARTHUR McCRAY
Gospelizer

"UNITY in Diversity Without ENFORCED Conformity"

—William Hiram Bentley

Collaboration & Integrity of Activist Black Believers

A Work-Watchword

How Collaborative Principle Preserves Integrity in Group Cohesion and Social Coalition

REV. DR. WALTER ARTHUR McCRAY
Gospelizer

BLACK LIGHT FELLOWSHIP
A Beacon of Christ

REV. DR. WALTER ARTHUR MCCRAY is a Gospelizer, a holistic "Good News messenger" of the resurrected Lord, Jesus Christ. A seasoned minister, writer, national speaker, and servant-leader of the Church, he resides with his wife in Chicago.

Unity in Diversity
Without Enforced Conformity
Collaboration & Integrity of Activist Black Believers

REV. DR. WALTER ARTHUR MCCRAY
Gospelizer

Address: P.O. Box 5369 • Chicago, IL 60680
Phone: 773.826.7790 • FAX: 773.826.7792
Website: www.blacklightfellowship.com
Email: info@blacklightfellowship.com

Editorial Services: Mary C. Lewis, MCL Editing, Etc., Chicago, IL
mclwriter@msn.com

Cover & Book Design: Michelle D. Muhammad, MDM Design, Chicago, IL
mdm@mdmdesign.biz
www.mdmdesign.biz

Printed in the U.S.A. 19 18 17 1 2 3 4 5

ISBN: 978-0-933176-27-0 Paper Edition
ISBN: 978-0-933176-28-7 eBook Edition

Printed on Acid-Free Paper.

To
Activist Black Believers

Contents

Contents (continued)

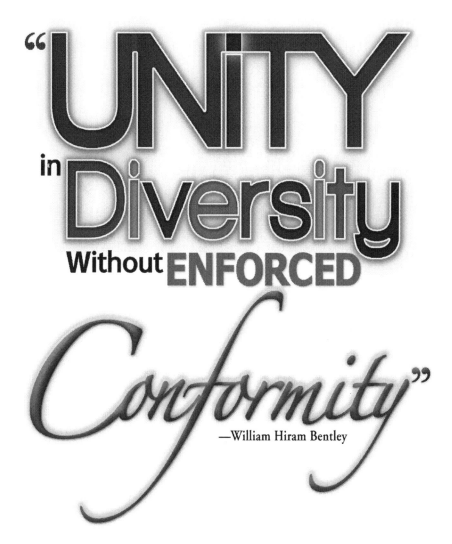

"UNITY in Diversity Without ENFORCED Conformity"

—William Hiram Bentley

1

COLLABORATIVE PRINCIPLE OF ACTIVIST BLACK BELIEVERS

"Unity in Diversity Without Enforced Conformity"

— William Hiram Bentley

THE CHALLENGE

Mission-minded and activist Black believers face a serious challenge: to minister for Jesus in alliances that effectively address a variety of social and systemic problems while maintaining our Christ-centered and cultural values.

Mounting political, cultural, and social crises are pressuring Black believers **to urgently strengthen or**

initiate collaborative endeavors to alleviate difficult and destructive problems, and to do so in the local, national, and global mission fields of our service. Our collective mission as African-descended followers of Christ is critical in these trying times. God's Spirit is calling and leading us to effectively work together to address the afflictions, social oppressions, and racial-cultural victimizations of African-descended people and a suffering humanity.

Growing evidence indicates that those who form broad-based alliances to address specific issues can sufficiently meet certain social needs.[1] Approaches of collective service—collaborations—are potent for alleviating social problems. They work better and make a greater impact than many "go-it-alone" endeavors.

> *Those who are sincere in their collaborative endeavors have earnest desires to stay faithful to Christ and their cultural identity.*

Heeding this trend, Black activist believers must utilize collaborative strategies, knowing that our people and others in need stand to benefit from the collective service approaches we use to effect social change. In one way or another, at the end of the day and amidst discussions about the current plight of the masses, **Black believers—and our people too—need to do some serious collaborating**. Therefore, I am encouraging Christian Blacks and our groups to foster collaborating ventures.

Yet, making social collaborations presents its own set of issues and problems for Black believers. **How to collaborate in public circles and keep our integrity** is the test confronting many Christians of African descent. Those who are sincere in their collaborative endeavors have earnest desires to stay faithful to Christ and their cultural identity. Many Black Christians need and seek informed and sensitive guidance to equip and arm themselves to successfully collaborate with integrity.

A WORK-WATCHWORD

In the spirit of Black believers working with one another and with others, and being true, I recommend a collaborative principle: **Unity in Diversity Without Enforced Conformity.** Here is a creative proverb of the late Rev. Dr. William Hiram Bentley that became the watchword of the NBEA, a collaborative Black Christian organization.[2]

"Unity In Diversity Without Enforced Conformity" is the wise saying of a sage. Here is a great maxim of *unity*, of *operational unity*. Here is a proverb embedded with *collective* interdependence, mutual leadership, and respected values. The motto seems to capture the true spirit of collaboration and integrity in a nutshell.

Since "watchword" means *"the core aim or belief of a person or group,"* it is accurate to intensify the description of the principle as a **"work-**watchword" to emphasize the idea of collaborating—**working together**—to give service to others. As explained below, the original adapters of this slogan used it to view and unite themselves in fellowship as **co-workers on a mission** for the kingdom of God. Laboring alongside genuine allies, they gave focus to their ministry by working hard and *righteously* to help Black people and their communities. The work-watchword facilitated a good understanding of their connected identity, and defined the personal limitations of their co-working relationship.

"Unity In Diversity Without Enforced Conformity" is a harmonizing slogan, and is especially apropos for bonding, and building bridges and networks of Black Christian persons and groups who pursue common goals. Moreover, it is vital for believers who form working relationships with those outside the Christian faith. The principle promotes the urgency for us to become co-working activists, and maintain our Black and Christian integrity in the process.

Perhaps the simplicity of *"Unity In Diversity Without Enforced Conformity"*—a profoundly powerful saying—is what heightens its value among good principles for collaborating which others utilize in various circles. I believe its terse expression makes it an *ideal* collaborative principle for unifying Black believers and guiding our partnering efforts.

As a concise saying, this work-watchword can easily become a driving force for Christians of African descent who seek social change. It can motivate those of us who take cooperative action to act with fidelity in the pursuit of fulfilling our God-given mission. While underscoring the importance of integrity, the principle helps Black believers to give greater collective service to a community experiencing crises.

For these reasons, believers of African descent should not hesitate to press this collaborative paradigm into practical service as we do Christ's work in the world. Black believers should wisely affirm the navigational character of this alliance-forming and integrity-protecting word. We should use the work-watchword to strengthen the interrelationships of Black believers, churches, and Christian groups. We should make the collaborative principle work for us. We should use it to undergird the holistic spiritual witness and unified social ministry we give, especially to classes of people who are poor, powerless, oppressed, and marginalized in our society and world.

The Backstory

African-American evangelical Bentley crafted *"Unity In Diversity Without Enforced Conformity"* in the late 1970s. He coined the work-watchword for an organization of predominantly African-American believers who desired to forge a collective interdependence in their Christ-centered ministry to people of African descent. Biblical and cultural integrity was in the forefront of their minds, and the global arena of missions was on their table.

Originally, the role of the slogan was to strengthen the bonds among members of a Christian group. God inspired the idea to help people in the group, workers and leaders in Christian churches and organizations, to band together in fellowship. Their purpose was to fulfill the charge of Christ's kingdom in special ministry to Black people. The group sought salvation, genuine community, survival, freedom, and empowerment for African-Americans in a nation of white racial stratification and oppression, and in a lost and suffering world.

When first formed, the motto envisioned and applied to a diverse but unified Black Christian collective whose individual associates would work for their causes and community. They participated alongside fellow Black believers and others who differed from one another in a variety of ways. These peace-loving believers freely chose *operational unity* as the strategic pathway to better achieve their common agenda. For the greater good of all, they each personally, peacefully, and freely submitted themselves to certain standards, values, and issues of their organizational working group, the National Black Evangelical Association (NBEA).[3] They collaborated, and most acted with integrity.

A BIBLICAL IDEA OF BLACKS

The cogent saying, *"Unity in Diversity Without Enforced Conformity,"* closely follows Christian theology in the Black experience. It is foremost a biblical idea created by a Black scholar of the Scripture.

Biblical teaching undergirds this work-watchword of activist Black believers. Both its call to collaborate and to be of integrity have roots in God's Word. The principle clearly applies Scripture instruction that identifies the community of believers (Christ's Church) as "one body" (**unity**) with "many members" (**diversity**) who relate to one another and work together with "freedom" that resists domination (**without enforced conformity**). (See, for example, Romans 12:4-5; Galatians 5:1, 13; and related passages.)[4]

As noted above, this biblically-based work-watchword arose from within a Black and Christian context. African-American believers advocated doing ministry with an intentional cultural emphasis, and within the oppressive social context of a not-so-friendly white, and white Christian, America. As such, this maxim of collaboration and integrity has come to us as an incipient expression of implicit Black theological thought, and liberating social action.

WISDOM AND VALUE

Expressing a great degree of wisdom, this work-watchword has definite value as a strategic educational tool for grounding, guiding, and guarding Black believers who pursue a peacemaking journey. By assisting us to appropriately unite and join forces with others to address complex social problems, it facilitates the collective work of Black believers for the best interests of God's kingdom.

First, **Bentley's collaborative principle nurtures group cohesion and social coalitions**. It implicitly encourages Black believers and Christian groups to share or

These peace-loving believers freely chose operational unity as the strategic pathway to better achieve their common agenda.

combine our resources to work collectively for social causes. It frames our co-working relationships—either to strengthen existing bonds between Black believers, or by provoking us to formally align with others in common purposes and actions to help the afflicted masses. Those alliances may be with other Black believers from different traditions, or with non-Black believers. In addition, these working relationships may be with members of other religions, or even with those who do not profess any religious affiliation.

Second, **NBEA's adopted work-watchword helps us as Black believers to preserve our integrity**. In its role of nurturing collaboration, this principle inherently acts as a safeguard, even as we step out to unify our base and to join with others in combined social efforts to change our communities and the world. The work-watchword of integrity applies when we collaborate either among ourselves or with others outside Christian circles. Integrity is essential in all personal and working relationships of Black believers.

Nearly four decades have passed since the creation of NBEA's unitive motto. Over the years, this work-watchword has grown in appreciation and increased in value for Black believers and Christian leaders. Men and women of Black Christian experience continue to promote this very practical collaborative idea. The principle is also very relevant for strengthening the progress of the wider black group, irrespective of faith or non-faith affiliations. The quest to achieve an optimum level of black unity and community in America—and in other areas of the

African Diaspora—continues to be a challenging goal for people of African descent and our leadership. Thus, the collaborative principle remains especially pertinent for Christian African-Americans, and then for black people throughout the world. I commend the work-watchword to them all for this unitive purpose. 🔲

2

COLLABORATION AND INTEGRITY

ANSWERING SOCIAL CRISES WITH COLLABORATION

Crises and Problems

The contemporary circumstances facing followers of Christ are rapidly and significantly changing, and are getting rougher. Vexing cultural problems, national distress, and global human crises characterize the social climate.[5]

Crises and Problems

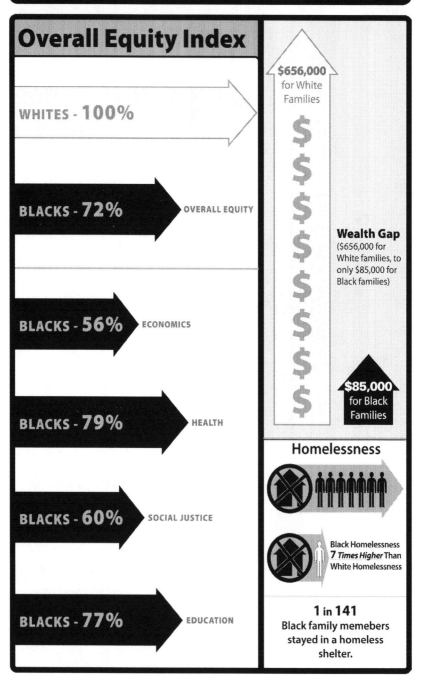

Overall Equity Index

WHITES - **100%**

BLACKS - **72%** — OVERALL EQUITY

BLACKS - **56%** — ECONOMICS

BLACKS - **79%** — HEALTH

BLACKS - **60%** — SOCIAL JUSTICE

BLACKS - **77%** — EDUCATION

$656,000 for White Families

Wealth Gap
($656,000 for White families, to only $85,000 for Black families)

$85,000 for Black Families

Homelessness

Black Homelessness **7 *Times Higher*** Than White Homelessness

1 in **141**
Black family memebers stayed in a homeless shelter.

Crises and Problems

- Black-on-Black violence • Mass incarceration of Black males • Law-enforcement violence and murders • High unemployment • White racism, nationalism, and privilege • Cultural and moral degeneration • Inferior schools • Lack of fresh water in Africa • Slavery and sex trafficking • Terrorism • Religious persecution • Mental illness • People lost without Christ • . . .

These social problems and crisis conditions also describe the mission field of Black believers, an already racially beleaguered group with relatively limited resources. Believers of African descent face a myriad of problems in the world God calls us to love and serve.

Sincere believers urgently desire to positively affect the lives of people who continually suffer. Many do all they can to substantially alleviate pressing problems by seeking to impact the social order. Yet, the ministries of many notable Christians, great churches, and good organizations still fall short of alleviating the vast needs of the afflicted masses. We need something more to effect greater social changes.

Opportunity

African-American believers face the taxing problems of an often soul-wearying social climate. Ironically, the rising tide of problematic cultural, national, and world crises has opened a door of opportunity for Black believers. God has redeemed people of African descent from slavery in America. African-Americans have already experienced the crucible of extreme suffering, and the salvation of divine deliverance. Our history is a witness that God is compassionate to deliver the oppressed from their oppression, and those who suffer from other afflictions of life—if we trust Him, together.

I believe that a *Kairos* moment—a divine season of opportunity—is present for Black believers to become a greater godly influence in the world. The Lord has especially prepared and positioned us as Black believers to address urgent needs in this very critical hour of humanity. God can mightily use us to effect transforming and reforming changes in the lives of people and communities throughout the Earth. Through faith-bathed and social activist ministry, we can make a lasting impact on the spiritual and social experience of our people, the nation, and the world.

> *Our history is a witness that God is compassionate to deliver the oppressed from their oppression*

If only . . . If only as believers of African descent we can continue to discover better ways to expand our working relationships with one another, and with others. If only we collaborate.

Collabortion

The word family "collaborate," "collaboration," "collaborative," and "collaborating" contains key terms that express the idea of **"jointly working together" as co-laborers**, the root meaning of collaborating. "Collaboration" easily interchanges with its synonymous partners, **"network," "coalition," "alliance," "partnership," "co-working association," "teamwork,"** etc. Respectively, each term has its own shade of meaning, characteristics, relevance, and special application when defining diverse groups of organized co-laborers in the social sphere.[6] "Collaboration" best describes the co-working relationship of these persons or groups.

A general overview shows that the relationship of collaborating parties or partners—whether individuals or groups—may be informal, semi-formal, or formal. Collaborators usually organize around common interests to achieve mutual goals. Their interactions with one another can be temporary or more lasting. The scope and means by which collaborators relate in various co-working relationships can span a wide spectrum: from basic **communication**, to **cooperation**, to **coordination**, to **co-working**, or to **contractual agreement**.

COLLABORATION

Definition

"The act or process of jointly working together"

Synonyms

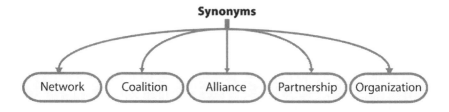

(Network) (Coalition) (Alliance) (Partnership) (Organization)

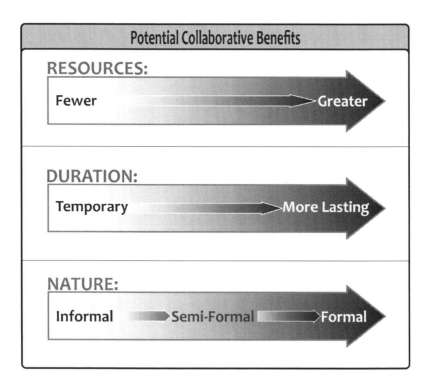

Potential Collaborative Benefits

RESOURCES:

Fewer ➤ Greater

DURATION:

Temporary ➤ More Lasting

NATURE:

Informal ➤ Semi-Formal ➤ Formal

Possibilities for a Wide-Ranging Scope of Relations and Work

(Communication) (Cooperation) (Coordination) (Co-Work) (Contract)

Black believers and our groups should participate in strategic collaborations somewhere along the wide spectrum of co-working relationships. Here there is room for creativity and flexibility as we work together. On the essential side, it is vital to clearly *communicate* with one another about our common concerns and issues. Black believers should inform and strategize with one another. On the "all-in" side, the crucial need to jointly tackle pressing problems will compel some of us to make *legal compacts*, and to exert the effective social and economic power that such vehicles afford.

ALLYING INTEGRITY WITH COLLABORATION

As African-descended followers of Christ, what kind of partnerships are good to form, or what kind of coalitions are appropriate to engage? Black believers are *in* the world but not *of* the world. Therefore, we are spiritually responsible for working with others and have a need to be "kept" by God in the process (cf. John 15:19; 17:11, 14-16). How to work with others in mutually beneficial ways without ever compromising our core beliefs is the crux of the matter—is integrity.

Black believers who collaborate with others show their integrity by being **trustworthy to their Christian and cultural core values and beliefs, without compromise. They stay Black and of Christ while collaborating with others.** Collaborative relationships of activist Black believers must always demonstrate their integrity. The critical task of African-descended followers of Christ is discovering the best ways to collaborate and keep acting with integrity by adhering to high moral principles. A good collaborative principle can help us to achieve this goal, and sustain our standards.

APPLYING UNITY, DIVERSITY, AND UNFORCED CONFORMITY

Following is a brief explanation of "unity," "diversity," and unforced "conformity" as these exist in a collaborative principle, and apply in a group setting of Black Christians.

> **Unity** in the work-watchword.

*"There is **one body** and one Spirit, just as you were called in one hope of your calling . . ."*
Ephesians 4:4, *NKJV* (emphasis added)

The *unity* of Black believers among themselves and with collaborating entities is *operational*, not absolute. We should not seek to unite around all things but on achieving simply stated common goals. Our *operational unity* aims toward achieving a clearly defined and greater good than any of the participating entities could attain in isolation of the others. *Operational unity* also makes room for the *collective* interdependence of associates, and a collective leadership model to fluidly guide the collaboration.

> **Diversity** in the work-watchword.

*"For as we have **many members in one body**, but all the members do not have the same function . . ."*
Romans 12:4, *NKJV* (emphasis added)

In this context, *diversity* recognizes and respects the *core distinctiveness* of each person or group that comprises the whole. None should downplay or disrespect collaborators' germane differences. The diversity of gifts is very beneficial for the collaboration. Each Black believer or Christian group should take care to maintain their specific focus of ministry to the persons or group God calls them to serve. The dynamics of a collaboration should not assimilate or neutralize the unique contributions of its diverse entities.

Unforced conformity in the work-watchword.

"Stand fast therefore in the liberty by which Christ has made us free, and do not be entangled again with a yoke of bondage."
Galatians 5:1, *NKJV* (emphasis added)

The **conformity** of a Christian Black individual or group is **unforced**, and never becomes absolutely binding in an association governed by a collaborative principle. Instead, the relationship always *preserves the freedom* of each entity to conform or not conform—**to engage or disengage**—in a specific matter as the occasion, issue, or conscience may require. Collaborating "**without enforced conformity**" helps to preserve integrity and nurture peacemaking in the group. In our partnering efforts, African-descended followers of Christ should always adhere to the crucial core affirmations of our biblical faith.[7] We should never relinquish certain essential values due to the pressure of collaborating partners.

3

COLLABORATORS: Peacemakers Gospelizing Peace

Biblical teaching helps this message to achieve its purpose: to motivate Black believers to collaborate, and to act with integrity when doing so. Scripture investigation uncovers an embedded idea of collaboration in Jesus' teaching on "**peacemakers**" in the seventh *Beatitude* (Matthew 6:9). Closely related is the early Church's prophetic summary of Christ's mission on Earth as the One who came "**gospelizing peace**" (Ephesians 2:17).

Following in the footsteps of our Lord, activist Black believers are inherently gospelizing and peacemaking collaborators. Christ has commissioned us to bring social healing, repair, and wholeness through cooperative good works. God desires to use the joint efforts of Black believers to effect social and systemic transformation (peace) in the holistic living experience of those who are most needful among us. Let's see how the Scripture ideas of *peacemaking* and *gospelizing* by Christ's disciples relate to the good works of collaborators.

THE PEACEMAKER'S BEATITUDE

As a collaborative principle written by a Bible-believing scholar, it is helpful to view *"Unity In Diversity Without Enforced Conformity"* in a biblical context. Here we turn to the blessed, peacemaking words spoken by our Lord in His *Sermon on the Mount.* Jesus set the standard of unified service for His followers by teaching them a *Beatitude*:

Christ has commissioned us to bring social healing, repair, and wholeness through cooperative good works.

"Blessed are the peacemakers, For they shall be called sons of God"
(Matthew 5:9, *NKJV*, emphasis added).

The Essence of Peacemaking

In the Jewish cultural context of the *Beatitude*, peacemakers bring the peace of *"Shalom."* The Hebrew word *"Shalom"* expresses the **peace** of great goodness in life that happens whenever and wherever the presence and rule of God prevails in human affairs. The *Shalom* idea of "peace" gathers within its scope **harmony, welfare, well-being, completeness, prosperity,** and **safety**. Thus, the peacemakers identified by Jesus are in fact ***Shalom-makers.***

Peacemakers belong to a divine and socially impactful class of humanity described in the *Beatitude* as "**sons of God**" (*huios theou*). Though not stated in a way that is gender-neutral, the literal phrase in this biblical passage is inclusive of both females and males.[8] It stresses the highest relationship of redeemed persons with God, women and men, and expresses their group identity and divine nature. Thus, peacemaking "sons of God" are **a community of reconciling agents or ambassadors who demonstrate God's effectual and socially transforming power in the world.** Peacemaking "sons of God" are proactive "peace-workers" or "*Shalom*-workers"—which gives a better understanding of their social mission.[9]

The peacemaking *Beatitude* of Jesus has two implications. First, the Lord calls believers themselves to live and fellowship together in peace. Otherwise, His followers simply prove that their peacemaking overtures are hollow and hypocritical. Peacemakers of Christ are inherently unifiers and workers of good, first and foremost among themselves. Jesus spoke these words to His disciples,

> "Salt *is* good, but if the salt loses its flavor, how will you season it? **Have salt in yourselves, and have peace with one another**"
> (Mark 9:50, *NKJV*, emphasis added).

Second, with their own unity and well-being intact, our Lord challenges His followers to peacefully work together doing good for others. They should bring to their world the peacemaking spirit, service and sacrifice of their unified and caring community. Jesus said to His disciples,

"You are the salt of the earth . . ."
(Matthew 5:13b, *NKJV*, emphasis added).

In the spirit of *Shalom*-peace, genuine **peacemakers** work to improve the overall quality and fortune of life for persons and groups who experience and receive their ministry. Peacemakers collaborate to address and alleviate germane human and societal problems by fostering social healing and wholeness—**peace**. The Lord pronounces His blessing upon these **"peacemakers"** by naming them **"sons of God"** for their cooperative peacemaking endeavors. God owns them as His true offspring. They are God's transforming social agents who surely reveal the divine attributes of His godly nature. Followers of Jesus embrace the peacemaking practice of "working together" with others for the benefit of those in need. Their collective forms of social ministry—peacemaking collaboration—pleases Christ and enjoys His blessing.

Peacemakers versus Peacekeepers

Careful students of Scripture note the difference between those who are "peace*keepers*" versus those whom Jesus blessed as "peace*makers*."[10] Peace*keepers* work through force to bring about the cessation of brawls and battles. They use power to maintain or restore civility and tolerance between persons or groups who were (or are) enemies, and who express hostilities toward one another. Peace*keepers* are primarily power-*mediators* for those who disagree, fight, act hateful, or make war. They use enough strength to keep tensions down and barriers up between antagonistic people. Depending on the approach they adopt, **sometimes peace*keepers* lose their integrity** in the process of doing their work.[11]

On the other hand, peace*makers* do far more than the limited work of peace*keepers,* those who forcefully provide a barrier between enemies. "**Peace*makers***" bring about peaceful conditions and circumstances for those in need. Their actions and works bring the likes of **social healing**, **wholeness**, **harmony**, and **prosperity** into the lives of others. By doing cooperative and extensive good works in the spirit and pattern of Christ, peace*makers* make life much better for those they serve. Their peace*making* practices bring well-being and good fortune into the lives of others. Moreover, peace*makers* work to restore broken relationships to harmony and friendship through fostering a genuine spirit of reconciliation.

On occasion, peace*keepers* may do some of the work of peace*makers.* But that is not their main concern. Peace*keepers* simply exert great influence, pressure, and power to keep

> *Followers of Jesus embrace the peacemaking practice of "working together" with others for the benefit of those in need.*

enemies at arm's length to prevent fights from erupting. It is very possible to be peace*keepers* without ever becoming peace*makers*.

However, peace*makers* can perform their ministry apart from acting as powerful *keepers* of the peace between warring parties who have conflicts, disagreements, and hostility. It is very possible to be peace*makers* without taking on the power-role of peace*keepers*. Moreover, the good works performed by peace*makers* often results in praise for their services. One fruit of their ministry is **the respect of their integrity in the eyes of the public**. Jesus said that peace*makers*—not peace*keepers* or even peace-*lovers*—will come to be known and recognized as genuine "sons of God."

In summary, four traits demonstrate the character of peace*makers*. *First*, they show their unified peacemaking mission. *Second*, they manifest sacredness and godly power to heal and repair unhealthy social conditions and relations; they bring safety, security, and a peaceful end to hostilities. *Third*, they evince the Lord's gracious favor—His blessing—upon their lives. *Fourth*, their reputation is one of divine integrity as measured by those who call their name: "sons of God."

CHRIST'S PEACEMAKING AND GOSPELIZING PEACE

The same biblical term in Matthew 5:9 that describes disciples of Christ as "peacemakers" (*eirenopoioi*) also describes the **peacemaking** work of Christ.[12]

"[19] For God was pleased to have all his fullness dwell in him, [20] and through him to reconcile to himself all things, whether things on earth or things in heaven, by **making peace** [*eirenopoieo*] through his blood, shed on the cross"

(Colossians 1:19-20, *NIV*, emphasis added).

Jesus is the **Peacemaker** *par excellence* through His atoning sacrifice—the blood He shed for humanity, and our sin, on the cross. Through Christ, God "**reconciles to himself all things**." The Lord has blazed the peacemaking trail for His followers.

Jesus is the "**Prince of Peace**" (Isaiah 9:6), and the mission of peacemaking characterized His life and work on Earth. The Scripture states emphatically that Jesus came "**gospelizing peace**" (Acts 10:36-39; Ephesians 2:17, literally). Leaders in the early Church used this phrase to summarize the complete life and ministry of Jesus. He was a *Gospelizer of peace*. A "Gospelizer" is a holistic "**Good News messenger**." Gospelizers speak **good words**, and do **gracious works** and **great workings** of God.[13]

Jesus brought to humanity the "**Good News**" (**Gospel**) **of peacemaking**, and demonstrated this divine grace and power wherever He did ministry. The Lord Jesus always proclaimed and effected peace in the spiritual, personal, social, and communal conditions of those He served. He offered the holistic peace of God to all who faced estrangement, affliction, misfortune, and oppression.

The words, works, and miraculous workings of Jesus effected peace (*Shalom*) in several dimensions:

• He gospelized the peace of personal reconciliation and friendship with God.

- He gospelized the peace of healing in our being, and contentment in our hearts.

- He gospelized the peace of cessation of hostility and the fostering of harmony in our relationships.

- He gospelized the peace of social well-being, prosperity, and wholeness in the experiences and circumstances of life.

Jesus ministered peace for the holistic benefit of those He served.

PEACEMAKING COLLABORATORS OF GOOD WORKS

Genuine peacemakers share the divine nature and follow in the sacrificial and reconciling footsteps of Jesus Himself. **Peacemakers are inherently Christ-commissioned collaborators.**

Jesus formed His disciples into a gospelizing community. By working together in cooperation with their Savior, they ministered the holistic peace of God to those in need. Essentially, the followers of Jesus—as the "sons of God"—collaborated with Him to gospelize His transformational peace in all dimensions of life (see Luke 8:1ff.).

Authentic ministry of peacemaking collaborators follows in the footsteps of Gospelizer Jesus (cf. Luke 4:18-19). Just as Jesus is a peacemaking Gospelizer, so also are His followers. As disciples of Jesus, **we too are Gospelizers of peace. As co-workers with our Lord,** we too are holistic Good News messengers of peace in the world. With Christ and other believers, **we too are collaborating peacemakers in the social order**. As the Church, we are a gospelizing community of peacemakers to our people and unto the ends of the Earth.

Peacemaking collaborators gospelize good works. The sufferings of humanity touch us and move us to action. By working with one another, we act to repair many social ills, and advocate for many vital and worthwhile human causes. Our common and cooperative goal is to effect social healing and wholeness. In unified ventures, we confront vexing social problems that comprise a long and open-ended list of labors that we do in the Name of our Lord for all who suffer affliction:

- opposing political policies of exclusion and violence • combating slavery and sex trafficking • fighting for social justice • standing against religious persecution • combating various forms of terrorism • making intercession and intervening in situations of actual or impending warfare and outbreaks of hostility between enemies • confronting the alarming tide of Black-on-Black violence and its systemic causes in urban areas such as Chicago • combating notions and realities of white supremacy and racism • battling white nationalism and privilege • protecting those who are "strangers" or immigrants • advocating for reparations • caring for and empowering the poor and the marginalized • reforming a criminalized justice system • securing housing for the homeless • creating job and employment opportunities • developing cooperative economic initiatives • simply feeding the hungry and giving water to the thirsty • interceding and intervening for those who find themselves in menacing distress • proclaiming the Gospel of God's grace, and the hope, salvation, and deliverance brought to humanity by Christ • etc.

Collaborating to perform these and comparable good works in God's world are the kind of gospelizing efforts by social activists that characterize divine collaborating peacemakers.

4

COLLABORATORS
OF
INTEGRITY

In our collaborative efforts, African-descended believers must wrestle with *integrity*.

INTEGRITY

Definition
Integrity is having strong and uncompromising moral principles and character.

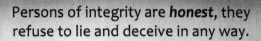

Persons of integrity are **honest**, they refuse to lie and deceive in any way.

They are **upright**, righteous and just.

Persons of integrity have **honor**, a high and careful regard for their profession.

They have **probity**, confirmation as tried and proven persons who adhere to the highest values and ideals.

They are **highly principled**, trustworthy and incorruptible.

Persons of integrity are **true** to their cultural trust and spiritual calling.

Activist Black believers of integrity are *faithful* as Black and Christian collaborators.

Several questions help to focus the issue of integrity for Black Christian collaborators.

• Faced with formidable cultural, political, economic, and human problems, is it ever advisable, or even mandatory, for an African-descended follower of Jesus to collaborate with those of differing traditions but like faith?

- To better confront and alleviate pressing social problems, should resource-driven Black believers choose to work alongside others in a pluralistic society and diverse world?

- If ever it is right for us to do so, should Black believers cross the belief-line to collaborate with persons and groups who have compatible agendas and greater resources, but differing beliefs?

I believe so. Provisionally.

To answer these questions, consider the relevance of *motivations*, *values*, *inner peace*, and *Jesus' Name* to the matter of maintaining integrity in collaboration.

MOTIVATIONS

Integrity in collaboration begins with righteous motives. When collaborators form alliances for proper reasons, they lay a foundation of integrity.

Some motivating values are inherently Christ-like. For instance, the desire to show love, serve others, and gospelize the poor fits this category. Christ-centered collaborators serve others rather than themselves. This means that as Black believers we should design our collaborations to benefit the least fortunate of the masses, not to enrich our personal coffers.

Other motivating dynamics also move Black believers to form collaborative relationships. Consider the following motives that inspire collaborative works: being faithful to God, having spiritual urgency, redeeming humanity, increasing service capacity, etc. With a desire to practice good works, African-American believers, churches, and Christian groups should respond to social cries and crises with an attitude of being faithful to God. Our loyalty to God must couple with a spiritual responsibility to care for and fully serve the present generation of our people, and a hurting humanity. Spiritual urgency should lead Black believers to make coalitions, to cooperatively join with others to form problem-solving alliances.

Jesus Christ—the Cornerstone of the Christian faith—eternally remains the same; He never changes; His compassion continues (Hebrews 13:8; Malachi 3:6; Lamentations 3:21-23). However, followers of the Lord will always make changes. That is, provided we desire to grow and stay pleasing unto God; so long as we aspire to effectively fulfill our God-given mission by compassionately redeeming a world that is constantly and drastically changing. The Lord calls His followers to change—to change our attitudes and ways; to change our approaches to doing ministry; to change and strengthen our strategies for service.

Many disciples of Christ and leaders of Christian ministries must change from a mindset of

> *Spiritual urgency should lead Black believers to make coalitions, to cooperatively join with others to form problem-solving alliances.*

individualism and extreme independence. As collaborating peacemakers, we should reject individualistic approaches to ministry and adopt models that provide *unified cooperative service* to those in need. As peacemaking disciples of Jesus Christ, we should open our minds to freely explore new ways of collaborating to increase our capacity in service.

As Black believers who are the peacemaking "sons of God," we should earnestly desire to coalesce in our mission to serve and redeem humanity. We should highly value teamwork. We should listen to the promptings of God's Spirit, leading us to expand our current alliances. Or, He helps us to develop fresh and resourceful networks that are social, cultural, economic, and strategic. The Lord expects no less from us. Practicing *"Unity In Diversity Without Enforced Conformity"* lays the foundation for these resourceful collaborative networks. The principle sets the rules of engagement for Black believers who create and contribute to these necessary coalitions.

VALUES

Protective Principle

Black believers can develop good alliances by using *"Unity in Diversity Without Enforced Conformity."* Practicing the principle enables us to form cooperative and successful working associations with others. As Black believers, we demonstrate integrity by holding to our personal values when working together with others. In this regard, the collaborative principle is pragmatic.

It is practical for watching over the integrity of Black believers in our social activist ministry for Christ.

The operative and protective phrase in the work-watchword is ". . . **without enforced conformity**," and provides any collaborator the freedom to choose a personally appropriate path for moving forward at any given time. Black believers decide when, when not, or how to freely conform in any collaborative endeavor. As a clear principle based on biblical truth, the work-watchword guides Black believers in forging pathways to collaborate with integrity. When understood and intentionally applied, the principle empowers sincere African-American Christians in our attempts to collaborate without compromising the essence of our values. The values we use to define and measure the preservation of Black Christian integrity are biblical, theological, spiritual, moral, and cultural. By adhering to the collaborative paradigm, we can protect our Christ-centered and Black identity.

Alliances—What's Beneficial?

Trying times—political, economic, cultural, and otherwise—compel Black believers to discover more successful ways to collaborate for the greater good with our brothers and sisters of like Christian faith. Christian-based coalitions assume the common ground of core beliefs, and offer a measure of theological and spiritual security to Christ's followers who participate in them. Otherwise, the issue of integrity raises a pressing question for collaborators who align with non-believers:

What form of alliances are beneficial for Black believers to engage while seeking to preserve their distinctive identity and mission?

Not every collaborative association *per se* is conducive to respecting or safeguarding Black Christian persons or groups. Though not without its own set of difficulties, it is one thing when we decide as Black believers to make needful adjustments to collaborate with other followers of Christ outside our immediate circle of fellowship. It is potentially quite a complicated or conflicting matter for us to align ourselves with non-believers in the public square.

Alliances with Non-Christians

The collaborative principle is useful for making interfaith collaborations of Black believers with non-Christian communities of faith and good will.

As necessary from time to time, Black believers will seek common ground for working with non-Christian persons and groups from diverse backgrounds, and those who do good works at home or in the global community. We may join social networks to cooperate with non-Christians of other religious beliefs, simply because they demonstrate their viability as worthwhile partners by seeking the common good (i.e., they have integrity), despite them not being Christian. For instance, when gathering to strategize in circles that are Jewish or Islamic, the idea of *operational unity* empowers Black believers to tackle common and pressing social problems through collaboration with these members of other religious entities.

Followers of Jesus may also find occasion to collaborate in circles characterized by non-faith constituents, with those who do not practice any formal religious beliefs. In doing so, some believers will recall the words of those who sing and dare to dream *"The Impossible Dream"*: these collaborators may choose *"... to be willing to march into hell for that heavenly cause."*[14]

Some Black believers have convictions against the practice of Christ's followers collaborating with non-faith entities. Perhaps we can encourage those naysayers by leading them around their mental, emotional, and spiritual stumbling blocks regarding the practice. We can help by teaching them biblical stories about persons of faith who worked together with non-believers in political relationships. Queen Esther, Daniel, Nehemiah,[15] and other persons of faith served—i.e., collaborated—in this capacity. They also accomplished great good for their people, and they kept their integrity.

Vigilance

When God leads Christian blacks to do peacemaking collaboration in a diverse or multicultural venue, **He constrains us to be vigilant in maintaining our integrity.** God has given us a charge to guard the Gospel and to be watchful for ourselves (cf. 1 Timothy 4:16; 6:14, 20; 2 Timothy 1:12-14; 4:5; Proverbs 4:23). Therefore, by standing strong in the Lord we must both guard the spiritual trust given to us by God, and cover our own backs. Jesus warned His disciples to "watch" and "pray" (cf. Mark 13:33; 14:38).[16]

We should be quick to prick the conscience of naïve or novice believers who are prone to move to collaborate too fast by warning them not to. They should not hastily minimize dangers associated with collaborative relationships between Christians and interfaith or non-faith entities. For instance, the subtle temptation for a believer to court religious syncretism is present in alignments formed with those of non-Christian beliefs or other religions.

Christians who amalgamate the teachings of Christ with the beliefs of a religion can dilute the distinctive character of the Christian faith. The practice can also reduce believers to impotency in our mission to redeem a lost world for our Savior, Christ the Lord. It is quite possible for salt to lose its flavor and its power to effect change—and to become worthless. **Savorless salt has lost its integrity** (cf. Matthew 5:13, Mark 9:49-50).

Shadrach, Meshach, and Abednego—the three Hebrew leaders who collaborated with the king of Babylon—faced the temptation to engage in the idolatrous practice of religious syncretism. But these godly leaders held firm to worship the God of their Hebrew experience and beliefs by refusing to bow down to the idolatrous golden image of King Nebuchadnezzar (cf. Daniel 3:12ff.). They kept their integrity.

By standing strong in the Lord we must both guard the spiritual trust given to us by God, and cover our own backs.

Black and Christian Fidelity

In all collaborative endeavors, followers of Christ should hold to their personal biblical beliefs and Christ-centered relationship. Integrity dictates that Black believers must resist the pressure to compromise exerted by a larger group, or by an entity with greater social and financial strength.

Our work-watchword never permits "enforced conformity." We must not allow others to control or co-opt our spiritual identity in Jesus Christ, or to subvert our redemptive mission in the world for the Lord, our Savior and Liberator. Neither as Christian Black individuals or groups must we ever permit the dominating aspects of white culture and white privilege to assimilate us or our cultural identity. Black believers must be and stay free.

The work-watchword helps to ensure that Black believers do not become traitorous "collaborators" with adversaries to Christ-centered faith and to the empowerment of African-descended people. In this way, Christian Blacks can use *"Unity In Diversity Without Enforced Conformity"* to **collaborate for good without collaborating with evil or the Enemy**.

Collaborators must first come to peace within themselves prior to peacefully working with others.

INNER PEACE

Integrity flows from peace within. Inward peace should govern Black believers when they choose whether to collaborate and with whom. Each one's conscience and personal conviction should determine their decision.[17] Collaborators must first come to peace within themselves prior to peacefully working with others. Black believers need personal faith and inner assurance when taking the step to become a member of a network, coalition, alliance, co-working association, partnership, or full collaboration.

I readily admit that the notion of Christians who collaborate, especially with interfaith or non-faith entities, disturbs some genuine believers. They look with suspicion or disdain on alliances between believers and non-Christians, despite the advantages and good outcomes the aligned entities can probably achieve by working together in such a relationship. On the opposite hand, other sincere believers in Christ will clearly see the value of the Christian–non-Christian alliance model, and are excited to co-align with it.

In response to either the "pro" or the "no" position of those who contemplate the scope of collaboration, Christian freedom says to every follower of Christ, "To each one, his or her own in the Lord." Each believer must first and absolutely choose the pathway that nurtures the peace of God within. Each follower of Christ should allow **the peace of God to rule in their heart** (cf. Colossians 3:15a). God's peace is the internal defining and affirming word for believers who collaborate.

Following the inner voice of one's spiritual peace is the bottom line for those who pursue working for Christ and serving humanity through peacemaking collaborations.

Keeping a good conscience, and not being conflicted when following the right path, are signs of the peace and integrity of a Black believer who collaborates.

IN JESUS' NAME

In the Name that is above all names—Jesus Christ the Lord—I encourage those of us who are believers of African descent to faithfully live the collaborative principle to help us fulfill our peacemaking directive for the present generation. I believe that the good Lord is leading (and perhaps is even **compelling**) His disciples to heartily apply *"Unity In Diversity Without Enforced Conformity"*—our work-watchword of integrity. In the Name of the **Prince of Peace**, we owe a great debt to God, our people, and humanity.

Integrity demands that we take care to fulfill our mission in the Name of the Lord Jesus Christ. Black believers must give Jesus the credit for our work as peacemaking collaborators. In all our collaborative works, we must faithfully represent and glorify Him— the aim and source of our life.

"[16]For **in him [Jesus Christ]** all things were created: things in heaven and on earth, and invisible, whether thrones or powers or rulers or authorities; all things have been created through him and for him.[17] He is before all things, and **in him all things hold together**.... [20] and through him [Jesus Christ] to **reconcile to himself all things**, whether things on earth or things in heaven, by **making peace** through his blood, shed on the cross" (Colossians 1:16-17, 20, *NIV*, emphasis added).

In union with Jesus—and in His Name—Black believers of integrity must do the work of collaborating peacemakers. The critical hour for our community and the crises of humanity are ever present. Christ urgently calls us to collaborate to meet the need, now. ❁

5

COLLABORATING CHURCH MEMBERS

COLLABORATION IN CHURCHES IS NATURAL AND PRIMARY

As a principle based on biblical teaching, *"Unity In Diversity Without Enforced Conformity"* has its first and most natural application within the membership of a local church. As noted earlier (see chapters 1 and 2), Scripture reveals the unity of the Church as "one body"; the diversity of the Church has "many members"; and the unforced conformity of Church members who protect their fellowship and working relationship as "freedom" from domination (see Romans 12:4-5; Galatians 5:1, 13). *"Unity In Diversity Without Enforced Conformity"* succinctly expresses the collaboration of church members with integrity.

A church setting is the primary place for all followers of Christ to collaborate. The season is present for members within African-American churches to form collaborating relationships with one another. I believe that Black believers who cut their co-working teeth in a local congregation will most likely become successful collaborators who effect social transformation. They first learn the value and lessons of collaborating with fellow church members. Then they use the principles and practices they've learned to initiate or join broader collaborative relationships with those of other churches and organizations.

BIBLICALLY, BELIEVERS ARE CHURCH CO-WORKERS

Clear biblical teaching specifically supports forming collaborative relationships in a church setting. The Scripture explicitly describes believers and their co-working relationship in the following ways:

1. Believers are in a "brotherhood/sisterhood" relationship: Jesus said, *"you are all brethren"* (Matthew 23:8b; see 23:8-12, *NKJV,* emphasis added). We are not in a master-servant relationship to one another. We are co-servants, Jesus is our Lord;

2. Believers are *"workers together"* or *"fellow workers"* i.e., "co-workers" or collaborators (1 Corinthians 3:9 and 2 Corinthians 6:1, *NKJV*, emphasis added);

3. Believers should practice *"submitting to one another in the fear of God"* (Ephesians 5:21b, *NKJV*; see 1 Peter 5:5, emphasis added). Mutual submission means all members listen to one another, and make consensual decisions;

4. Believers respect and listen to *"those who lead us"*—a unified group of **plural** leaders in church relationships, overseers who really care for the souls of their members (Hebrews 13:17, *NKJV*, emphasis added).

5. Believers practice *"liberty"* (freedom) in things non-essential in the faith (Galatians 6:1, 13, *NKJV*, emphasis added). We are free and called to live as free persons. Our freedom does not allow us to practice personal license or group legalism, but to serve others (1 Corinthians 6:12, 23; Romans 14:14-19; Galatians 2:4; 1 Peter 2:16);

6. Believers develop *"partnership"* in our working relationships, as a significant expression of *Koinonia* (Philippians 1:5, *NIV*; Philemon 6, 17, emphasis added).

The church that applies biblical teaching about co-working church relationships, will enjoy flourishing, collaborating relationships among its membership. Church members will discover freedom to work together, and to offer the best of their gifts and service to the Body.

KOINONIA IN CHURCH COLLABORATION

Church is not primarily a corporate structure, and its members certainly should not function as a drama-filled organization. Based on biblical teaching, true Church is essentially a *Koinonia*, a fellowship-community (see, Acts 2:42; 1 Corinthians 10:16; Philippians 1:5; and related passages). Believers who highly value genuine fellowship-community also value collaboration.

Pro-activist Black believers who desire to do Church as genuine fellowship-community will adjust their thinking to embrace the following values:

- **relating in a communal model as the Body of Christ**, rather than in a hierarchical, authoritarian model of Church order as a corporation;

- **encouraging mutual gift sharing in the freedom of the Spirit**, rather than restricting the full exercise of God's spiritual gifts in the Body, or limiting their expression by only certain persons or groups;

- **forming leadership paradigms that are collective, diverse, mutually submissive,**

consensual, and focused in service and sacrifice for others, rather than perpetuating leadership models that are autocratic and lording over people;

- **uplifting God-created male/female roles and relationships of spiritual equality and mutuality,** rather than those based on subservience;

- **providing avenues for full communal participation and empowerment,** rather than impeding or preventing opportunity for service based on unnecessary or non-essential standards such as age, socio-economic class, etc.;

- **consecrating, centering, and fully serving the poor and afflicted,** rather than marginalizing them in the fellowship-community.

Most believers desire a church of integrity. They tire of foolishness, irrelevance, and "not keeping it real." Doing church as fellowship-community (*Koinonia*) is doing church with integrity, and this biblical practice generates a spirit of collaboration among the members.

Church members who energetically practice *"Unity In Diversity Without Enforced Conformity"* will witness the growth and expansion of their fellowship-community, of their collaborative *Koinonia*. In their church, they will receive and cultivate **redeeming love**, **respect**, **unique** value, **belonging**, **ownership**, and the **empowerment** to influence, shape, and grow their church. Genuine believers thrive in a church environment **whose members demonstrate integrity and collaborate** with one another.

COLLABORATION FOLLOWS CHURCH HEALING

Moving church members toward forming collaborative relationships requires laying the groundwork of **personal and relational healing**. Black believers who receive healing find it much easier to work together when there is genuine peace in relationships. Whenever healing occurs among church members, collaborative relationships will naturally follow and spread through the congregation. And when church members collaborate in the power of the Holy Spirit, the fruit is church transformation.

Church Hurt

Some church members do not function well because someone has hurt them, or some bad thing that happened in a church setting has wounded their spirit. These wounds may be recent, or they may have occurred in years past. Nevertheless, the hurt is real and sensitive. The words of a popular saying express the true, but bitter, experience of many Christians: **There is no hurt like church hurt**.

The wounded heart and life of church members often cause major problems to the fellowship. Wounded church members may become reticent and withdrawn. They can become obstructionists to the process of forming wholesome group relationships with their Brothers and Sisters. Wounded members may even hinder the church from effectively performing its outreach services. All it takes is one influential wounded saint to cause bitter disruption in the unity and peace of the Body. One sour church member can wreak havoc to the best well-intentioned church service or program (see Hebrews 12:14-15).

Church leaders should prioritize the church program to seriously deal with issues related to **offenses, confrontation, forgiveness, repair, restoration, healing,** and genuine **reconciliation**. Otherwise, effective collaboration in the church simply will not happen. An unhealed and unhealthy church will not be able to sustain its collaborative momentum or long-term initiatives.

Any church that fails to minister to its wounded members, but allows open sores to fester in the fellowship-community, is a church that undermines its unity and subverts its mission. In this regard, an irresponsible body of believers—one that neglects the ministry of peacemaking—**forfeits the integrity** of its Christ-centered fellowship, and neutralizes its power as a godly community of Christ's peacemaking collaborators. Jesus said, **"Blessed are the peacemakers, For they shall be called sons of God"** (Matthew 5:9, *NKJV*, emphasis added). Jesus said, **"Have salt in yourselves, and have peace with one another"** (Mark 9:50, *NKJV*, emphasis added).

A good-faith attempt to collaborate church members can certainly gain traction in a congregation. But only if pastoral and lay leaders give due diligence to healing the wounds and broken relationships of church members.

Church Healing

In this spirit, the leaders who are responsible for church organization should place an emphasis on peacemaking in the Body. I recommend that they **develop a collaborative peacemaking team** for the church. The team should be representative of the entire membership, and tasked with the sole responsibility of bringing peacemaking ministry to the congregation. A pastor cannot do it all, and should not try to do it alone. Gifted ministers must **equip the saints** to do the work of peacemaking ministry (see Ephesians 4:12ff.).

Responsible church leaders should give form and organizational structure to the team of collaborating peacemakers, whose peacemaking goal should aim to heal broken lives and relationships. They should sanctify its members in the eyes of the congregation, and install them in a designated church service. Through prayer, teaching, special instructions, clear guidelines, and professional consultation, they should equip this peacemaking group of saints

An unhealed and unhealthy church will not be able to sustain its collaborative momentum or long-term initiatives.

to uplift and work for unity, harmony, and reconciliation—peace—among members of the Body. As needed cases emerge, assign the following situations to the care of these peacemakers: wounded church members, cases of offense, and problematic situations. Adequately resource and empower the peacemaking group to effect holistic healing in the lives of their Brothers and Sisters in Christ.

God spiritually empowers a collaborating and transformed church to work alongside other churches to transform their community. He also enables these peacemaking collaborators to exert a deeper and wider influence in our society and the world. Through their *"Unity in Diversity Without Enforced Conformity,"* these empowered collaborators will make a significant impact on their generation, in the Name of Christ.

Jesus said,
"A new commandment I give to you, that you love one another; as I have loved you, that you also love one another. [35] **By this all will know that you are My disciples**, if you have love for one another"
(John 13:34-35, *NKJV*, emphasis added).

Jesus prayed,
" 'I do not pray for these alone, but also for those who will believe in Me through their word; [21] that they all may be one, as You, Father, *are* in Me, and I in You; that they also may be one in Us, **that the world may believe that You sent Me** '"
(John 17:20-21, NKJV, emphasis added).

6

COLLABORATIVE URGENCIES OF ACTIVIST BLACK BELIEVERS

Black Americans face many crucial issues which all demand the unified engagement of Christian persons and groups of African descent. Below are several of the many issues which Black believers should consider urgent and worthy of our collaborative efforts.

Creating Space for Black Millennials in Church

Due to rapidly changing cultural and social experiences, there is a growing need in Black churches to apply the collaborative model to our working relationships. African-American young adults especially need to worship and serve in settings that promote collaboration. The current generation of Black young adults does not respond well to autocratic and domineering leadership models, church models notwithstanding.

Millennials think and behave in ways that are rather independent. Their social and spiritual style does not blindly and readily yield to following the "Just do what I say"-type of leader. Though some church leaders use authoritarian hierarchal forms of local church governance, these models often severely impede the development of genuine fellowship-community and effective work in a church. Solitary leadership models tend to have the same effect. Time and again, these types of leadership models drive away many Black young adults, or turn off those who are potentially church members.

Pastor and ministers, church elders, and stakeholders—these leaders are responsible for creating collaborative spaces in the church for Black millennials. Leaders of a local congregation would do well to apply fresh thinking on how best to reorder the operations of their churches. They should reconsider how to refashion relationship meetings for church members, reorganize leadership models, and establish effective organizational structures. And they should move to do so quickly.

Why?

The **obvious absence of the Black young adult age group** from many churches is telling, and testifies to serious problems with many churches. Their nonattendance on Sundays or through the week is unsettling. So is their absence from tracks to becoming a church leader, and their lack of access to giving input or having significant influence.

Foreboding thoughts often occur when we contemplate the spiritual and social future of Black American Christianity and our community when our Black Christian young adults are scarce in most churches. What happens to Black churches where Black young adults and youth are few or insufficient for the workload? What will become of the state of the souls and the whole of Black people in America when so many of our churches lack the social and spiritual strength of their Black millennials?

Black churches must earnestly and urgently collaborate with Christian Black young adults.

Transforming Poor Black Urban Communities

Black churches and believers of African descent must cooperate and purpose to transform the life experience of our Black and poor brothers and sisters. We can fulfill this mission by finding more effective ways to increase intra-faith collaboration, especially on the local urban level. This is to say that Black believers in their local communities and inner-city neighborhoods should cooperatively join with fellow Christian believers from various church and denominational traditions. There is little doubt that Black Christian believers and churches who collaborate can make a major difference in improving the quality of life for the poor and the least in their geographic communities.

Many of our people in urban settings depend on African-American churches as their last net of hope for security, support, and survival, especially in these times of anti-Black and poor social sentiments and policies. God admonishes His people that we should never turn our backs on our own flesh and blood (see Isaiah 58:7). Black believers who are socially and economically more fortunate than others must collaborate to minister to the poor and least among our people.

Local churches of different denominations or affiliations—those who share a close location in urban settings—should collaborate. By doing so they can significantly impact the quality of life for poor and underserved residents in their local areas. When small churches in proximity join their congregations in a working relationship as a unified "people of God"—for the cause of helping their immediate neighbors—God can cause great things to happen for Black urban dwellers throughout the nation.

African-American congregations that locally collaborate as peacemaking "sons of God" can bring about better and greater changes in the lives and experience of urban Black populations. Perhaps such alignments can generate authentic **revival**, which has both spiritual and *social* dimensions. Prayer, holistic gospelizing, repentance, personal transformation, and **social reformation by collaborating to impact the well-being of the masses** are essential ingredients of biblical revival (see Isaiah 58:6ff.). Black believers and churches who collaborate to effect change in the social arena demonstrate genuine revival. Their corporate works enhance the integrity and witness of the Christian faith in the Black experience in our communities, the nations, and the world.

God admonishes His people that we should never turn our backs on our own flesh and blood (see Isaiah 58:7).

COMBATING WHITE EVANGELICAL RACISM

The historical origin of *"Unity In Diversity Without Enforced Conformity"*—that is to say, the Christ-centered and Black cultural roots of its creator—makes this powerful saying especially commendable to mission-minded and activist Black believers, and to their non-Black allies. The *modus operandi* which the work-watchword highlights continues to urge earnest collaboration of African-descended evangelicals with one another amidst white evangelicalism and manifestations of racism. Its application by Black believers in this group is of utmost necessity, especially in the present political climate.

Considering the outcome of the 2016 U.S. presidential election, an astounding and disheartening 81% of white evangelicals voted for a candidate whose innumerous practices is their moral opposite.[18] And the voting pattern of these conservative white believers was in stark contrast and opposition to the votes cast both by most explicit Black evangelicals *and* by implicit Black evangelicals in African-American churches. Most Black evangelicals—stated and incipient—voted vastly different than white evangelicals.

Thus, in the current socio-political climate of white nationalism, and facing the apparent anti-Black sentiment of most white evangelicals, it is imperative that Black evangelicals coalesce around *"Unity In Diversity Without Enforced Conformity".* Black evangelicals must join forces to combat white evangelical racism. Working together in unity as Black believers across the wide spectrum and affiliations of Christian faith, we must develop effective strategies for countering an onslaught of policies and practices against the lives and well-being of Blacks. We must resist the perpetuation of anti-Black political policies and social practices whether they originate from Christians of whatever stripe, from haters, or from others.

In our peacemaking and collaborating mission for Christ, Black evangelicals must also do our part in providing a haven for other people of color, and for those who are the least and most vulnerable in American life. Collaborative practices of Black believers must allow space for non-Black persons and groups to align with us. There are progressive believers of non-Black racial and ethnic groups who desire honest relationship. They want to repair and nurture respectful, just, and empowering relations with Black people, and to raise the fallen and hurting of humanity.

We must provide sincere non-Black persons and groups the opportunity to work with Black believers, **and to follow the lead of Black believers in the collaborative group or venue**. Specifically, the time has long arrived for white Christian leadership to yield and submit themselves and their white privilege to the leadership of their brothers and sisters of African descent. Period. White believers who listen and learn to follow the leadership of Black Christians help to affirm the cultural and spiritual integrity of African-descended followers of Christ. 🞕

Notes

[1] For example, see:
- Cameron Conaway, Collaboration: Solving complex social problems through collaboration, *Harvard Business Review,* June 2015.
  https://hbr.org/2015/06/solving-complex-social-problems-through-collaboration
- Holly Watson, Power of collaboration, *CU Insight,* June 20, 2014.
  https://www.cuinsight.com/power-of-collaboration.html
- TED: Ideas worth spreading – "The Power of Collaboration" - great things happen when we work together. Whether on the web or in the face of disaster, these talks reveal the undeniable strength of teaming up.
  https://www.ted.com/playlists/431/the_power_of_collaboration
- Megan Conley, The power of teamwork: 31 quotes that celebrate collaboration, *Hubspot,* March 7, 2016.
  https://blog.hubspot.com/marketing/teamwork-quotes

Following is a sampling of several impactful collaborations, accessed 5/11/17:
- **Kinetic Response**; product of Kinetic Data which promotes collaboration for change management and problem resolution.
  http://kineticslive.com/
- **Samuel DeWitt Proctor Conference**;
  http://sdpconference.info/
- **The Leaders Network (Chicago)**;
  http://leadersnetworkchicago.org/
- **Circle of Protection**; Christian leaders organized to end hunger and poverty.
  http://circleofprotection.us/
- **W. K. Kellogg Foundation** (WKKF), **Truth, Racial Healing & Transformation**
  http://www.dayofracialhealing.com/ and
  https://www.wkkf.org/what-we-do/racial-equity/truth-racial-healing-transformation
- **Live Free USA**
  http://www.livefreeusa.org/
- **The Africa Study Bible**
  http://www.oasisint.net/#about

[2] The motto *"Unity in Diversity Without Enforced Conformity"* was crafted for the **National Black Evangelical Association** (1963, http://The-NBEA.org) by one of the organization's co-founders and Black evangelical statesmen, the **Reverend Dr. William Hiram Bentley.** Read his explanation of "Collective Interdependence: Black Operational Unity and Collective Leadership" in McCray, *Pro-Black, Pro-Christ, Pro-Cross: African-Descended Evangelical Identity* (Chicago: Black Light Fellowship, 2012), 29-34.

> https://www.blacklightfellowship.com/ Accessed 5/11/17.

See Bentley's original source: "Preface to the Second Edition," notes 3-4 in *The National Black Evangelical Association: Reflections on the Evolution of a Concept of Ministry* (Chicago: National Black Christian Students Conference, 1979, rev. ed.), 5-6.

[3] See the website for The National Black Evangelical Association.
> http://The-NBEA.org

[4] See the following references for instruction on unity, diversity, and freedom in the Church: 1 Corinthians 8:9; 9:1, 19; 10:29; 12:12-14, 20, 27; Romans 12:4-8; 2 Corinthians 3:17; Galatians 2:4; 3:28; 5:1,13; Ephesians 4:1-7ff.

[5] See the following sources for the data documenting different crises, accessed 5/11/17:
> http://www.msnbc.com/msnbc/the-state-black-america-national-urban-league-word-crisis
> http://money.cnn.com/2016/08/09/news/economy/blacks-white-wealth-gap
> http://soba.iamempowered.com/2016-report
> http://www.huffingtonpost.com/2012/03/06/black-families-homeless_n_1324290.html

[6] See, for example, the following; accessed 5/11/17:
- Types of Collaborations: Networks, Alliances, Coalitions, Partnerships, Full Collaboration
  http://www.ohcc-ccso.ca/en/courses/community-development-for-health-promoters/module-three-community-collaboration/types-of-col

- Collaboration, Coalition, Networks: What's the difference?
  http://arilikeairy.org/collaboration-coalition-networks-whats-the-difference/

- Coalitions, Consortia, and Partnerships
  http://www.encyclopedia.com/education/encyclopedias-almanacs-transcripts-and-maps/coalitions-consortia-and-partnerships

  - Evaluating networks, partnerships, collaborations, coalitions
    http://www.betterevaluation.org/en/node/1582

[7] See McCray, *Pro-Black, Pro-Christ, Pro-Cross*, 220ff., for a discussion of eight indispensable tenets of Christ-centered Black evangelical faith.

[8] *huios theou* "sons of God" is the literal, correct translation. See also Luke 20:36; Romans 8:14, 19 and Galatians 3:26. The *KJV* translates "children of God", which is not the literal phrase. See also *tekna theou* "children of God" in John 1:12; Romans 8:16, 21; 1 John 3:1, 2, 10; 5:2.

[9] See, for example, Walker, W. L. (1915). Peacemaker. In J. Orr, J. L. Nuelsen, E. Y. Mullins, & M. O. Evans (Eds.), *The International Standard Bible Encyclopaedia* (Vol. 1–5, pp. 2293–2294). Chicago: The Howard-Severance Company.

[10] For example, see the following: Morris, L. (1992). *The Gospel according to Matthew* (pp. 100–101). Grand Rapids, MI; Leicester, England: W.B. Eerdmans; Inter-Varsity Press; or Barclay, W. (Ed.) (1976). *The Gospel of Matthew* (Vol. 1, pp. 108–110). Philadelphia, PA: The Westminster John Knox Press.

[11] "In the name of peacekeeping, many compromise and lose their integrity in the process." See
  http://christiancommunitychurcharklow.hdpm.org/peacemakers-not-peacekeepers-part-1/ Accessed 5/11/17.

[12] *eirenopoioi*, "peacemakers" in Matthew 5:9, and "making peace" in Colossians 1:20 (*NIV*). The term only appears in these two places in the New Testament. "The substantive εἰρηνοποιοί, "peacemakers," of the seventh beatitude occurs only here in the NT (the verb of the same stem occurs in Col 1:20)." Hagner, D. A. (1998). *Matthew 1–13* (Vol. 33A, p. 94). Dallas: Word, Incorporated. Compare James 3:18.

[13] "The name **Gospelizers** brings together into one concise term **the holistic nature of believers' witness.** An authentic and

holistic Christian witness and mission show up in **good words**, in **gracious works**, and in **great workings** of God (all powerful and miraculous). Communication, demonstration, and transformation demonstrate a true Gospel witness." See McCray, *Gospelizers! Terrorized and Intensified* (Chicago: Black Light Fellowship, 2002), 3, 46, 50, 54, 57.

[14] "The Impossible Dream (The Quest)," music by Mitch Leigh, with lyrics by Joe Darion, 1965.

[15] Queen Esther served King Xerxes (King Ahasuerus) of Persia (Esther 1:1ff.; 2:7ff.); Daniel served King Nebuchadnezzar and King Belshazzar of Babylon (Daniel1:1, 6ff.; 5:1ff.); Nehemiah served King Artaxerxes of Persia (Nehemiah 1:1; 2:1).

[16] See Matthew 26:41; Mark 13:37; Luke 21:36; Ephesians 6:18.

[17] Cf. Romans 14:5; 1 Corinthians 10:29.

[18] William Galston, "Has Trump caused white Evangelicals to change their tune on morality?" FixGov (blog), Brookings Institute, October 19, 2016.
> https://www.brookings.edu/blog/fixgov/2016/10/19/has-trump-caused-white-evangelicals-to-change-their-tune-on-morality/   Accessed 5/11/17.

Also, Gregory A. Smith, "Among white evangelicals, regular churchgoers are the most supportive of Trump"
> http://www.pewresearch.org/fact-tank/2017/04/26/among-white-evangelicals-regular-churchgoers-are-the-most-supportive-of-trump/   Accessed 5/11/17.

About the Author

Rev. Dr. Walter Arthur McCray is a *Gospelizer*, a holistic *"Good News" messenger* of the resurrected Lord, Jesus Christ. He is a Chicago-based writer and entrepreneur, a seasoned servant-leader in the Church, and president of the *National Black Evangelical Association* (Chicago). **Dr. McCray** and his wife of 40+ years have several spiritual children, and God-children.

Contact:
773.826.7790
wamccray@blacklightfellowship.com